The ultimate business skills collection from Bloomsbury Business

The new *Business Essentials* series from Bloomsbury Business offers handy pocket guides on a wide range of business topics – from writing a CV and performing well in interviews, to making the most impactful presentations, finding the right work/life balance, brushing up your business writing skills, managing projects effectively, and becoming more assertive at work.

Available from all goo
as well as from

BLOOMSBU

Manage Projects Successfully

How to make things happen on time and on budget

BLOOMSBURY BUSINESS

LONDON • OXFORD • NEW YORK • NEW DELHI • SYDNEY

BLOOMSBURY BUSINESS
Bloomsbury Publishing Plc
50 Bedford Square, London, WC1B 3DP, UK
29 Earlsfort Terrace, Dublin 2, Ireland

BLOOMSBURY, BLOOMSBURY BUSINESS and the Diana logo are trademarks
of Bloomsbury Publishing Plc

First published in Great Britain in 2005 by Bloomsbury Publishing Plc
Revised edition published in 2009 by Bloomsbury Publishing Plc
(under the A&C Black imprint)
This revised and updated edition published in 2022 by
Bloomsbury Publishing Plc

A catalogue record for this book is available from the British Library

Library of Congress Cataloguing-in-Publication data has been applied for

ISBN: 978-1-3994-0227-9; eBook: 978-1-3994-0226-2

2 4 6 8 10 9 7 5 3 1

Text design by seagulls.net

Typeset by Deanta Global Publishing Services, Chennai, India
Printed and bound in Great Britain by CPI Group (UK) Ltd, Croydon CR0 4YY

To find out more about our authors and books visit www.bloomsbury.com
and sign up for our newsletters

Contents

Are you a good project manager?

Answer the questions and work out your score. Then read the guidance points to find out how you can improve your project-management skills.

What skills does project management require?

a. Being an all-rounder with an ability to see the 'big picture'.

b. Nothing special: a cool head, common sense and good organization will see you through!

c. A general understanding of the process and good management skills.

What does the word 'project' mean for you?

a. A finite task with a set cost and timescale.
b. Something that's difficult to accomplish.
c. It's just another word for ordinary work.

Do you feel you use your time effectively at work?

a. Yes. I am completely in control of my time.
b. I mostly stay on top of my work but occasionally run into problems.
c. No. I am completely snowed under.

Do you prioritize your work?

a. Yes. I make sure that I spend my time on important activities.
b. I try to but sometimes find my to-do list over-full.
c. Not really. I just do what grabs my attention.

Are you able to delegate?

a. Yes. I use my team effectively as I cannot be everywhere at once.
b. I do delegate but I find it hard.
c. No. I'd rather do things myself.

How do you rate your team management?

a. Good. I run a tight ship.
b. Not bad. There's room for improvement.
c. Help! My team is a nightmare – I can't control them!

Planning is:

a. One of my best skills.
b. A necessary activity, which I find difficult.
c. A waste of time.

Something unexpected happens. How do you react?

a. I keep calm as I've thought in advance about potential problems.
b. I'm normally surprised, but I'll deal with it.
c. I tend to panic.

a = 1, b = 2, c = 3. Now add up your scores.

Chapter 1 will be useful for everyone, as it summarizes the essentials of project management. Then, depending on your total score, the most relevant chapters are indicated below.

8–13: Well done; you have great project-management skills. There's always something you can learn, though, so look at Chapter 4 for ways to work with key sponsors – they can make your job a lot easier. Also, Chapter 5 offers useful tools, such as Gantt charts, which will help with organization.

14–19: You're getting there, but could do with polishing up your skills. Chapters 2 and 3 will help you manage yourself and others better. Chapter 5 is full of invaluable advice on planning, while Chapter 6 will help you cope better in emergencies.

20–24: You need some help with your management skills, but don't worry! Chapter 2 can help you improve your time management and Chapters 3 and 6 provide advice on building your team. Once you've mastered the basics, move on to Chapters 5 and 6 to fine-tune your planning.

1
Understanding the basics of project management

'Project management' is a term that's often bandied about today. It first became popular in the early 1960s, driven by businesses that realized that there were benefits to be gained from organizing work into separate, definable units and from co-ordinating different kinds of skills across departments and professions. One of the first major uses of project management was to handle the US space programme, and governments, military organizations and the corporate world have all since adopted the discipline. In this book, we'll be looking at how project management works and how you can take the stress out of it, whatever the size of the task at hand.

Although the term is now universally familiar, not that many people fully understand exactly what project management involves. We tend to think of it as common sense, and that anyone can manage anything by being calm and well-organized. These are qualities that a project manager definitely needs, but other things are essential too. Project management is, in fact, a structured way of working and recording events that can bring order and coherence to any set of tasks with a predetermined goal. This chapter sketches the outlines of that structure.

Step one:
Define what a project is

'Project' is one of those terms that is defined in various different ways by different bodies. However, all sources seem to agree that a project is:

> a task or set of tasks undertaken within specific timescales and cost constraints in order to achieve a particular benefit

The three stages

Think about the following:

- arranging a holiday;

- decorating a room;

- assembling a garden shed;

- moving house;

- organizing a party.

These are all examples of a project because they all have three things in common. In each case, you:

✓ Identify a need or benefit first of all.

✓ Start to produce whatever will satisfy the need.

✓ Use, operate or simply enjoy the fruits of your labours once all the work has been done.

This basic three-stage cycle is common to all projects, large and small, whether you're producing a physical product (such as a bridge or computer system), an event (like a product launch or sporting event) or a change in circumstances (an office move or reorganization, for instance).

The three parameters

In addition to the three stages, all projects have three key parameters (or factors) that have to be taken into account:

- time
- cost
- quality (also referred to as 'performance' or 'specification')

The relationship between these three elements is often shown as a triangle.

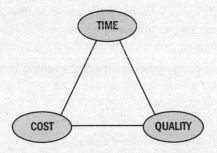

This is because, throughout the life of a project, the three factors are likely to come into conflict with one another. You will nearly always find that everyone wants high performance within a very short time, at minimum cost! However, if any one of these factors is absolutely essential, the other two will have to give way to a certain extent – it's impossible to be in all three corners at once, so you have to set priorities for the project, whatever it is.

Say, for example, your project had been to launch a new website for your business. Your priorities would probably have been in the following order:

- time – you'd have needed to get the new content and design ready for the launch as well as promotions and teasers to announce the new site;

- Quality – it would have been essential that everything was tested and worked properly when the website went live;

- cost – you might have had to spend whatever was necessary to make sure the other two parameters were met.

When you're beginning a new project, it's a useful exercise to place it within this triangle to indicate how flexible – or not – you could be with any of the three parameters.

So, from a combination of the three stages and the three parameters, we can see that a project:

- has a finite and defined life span;

- aims to produce a measurable benefit or product;

- contains a corresponding set of activities designed to achieve that benefit or product;

- has a defined amount of resources allocated.

The structure

The final, vital, requirement is that the project also has a proper organizational structure with defined responsibilities, so that everyone involved knows what they are doing and why; how it must be done; and by when.

> **TOP TIP**
>
> One important thing to bear in mind is that projects are finite – they will have a definite beginning and end. If these are unclear, and if you and others are working away without a proper goal in sight, it's not a project.

Step two:
Understand what project management is

All projects, large or small, are set up to create something new to an organization, and as a result, they create an environment that is unstable and risky.

Without change, though, we'd stagnate. Projects help us to develop, but it's important to keep them under tight control so that they stay focused and achieve what they're supposed to. This is where the project manager comes in!

The whole project management process revolves around three main areas.

Business

Projects must support your organization's business strategy. If they don't, they shouldn't be started in the first place. To work out whether a project is a good idea or not, there has to be agreement from everyone involved or affected about:

- what the project is;
- what its targets are;
- the benefits to the business.

It's the project manager's job to make sure the project has been properly defined and planned from the outset.

People

Projects revolve around people, and if the project manager isn't managing the team doing the work and all the other stakeholders, he or she isn't managing the project. Identifying or appointing certain people is also key, such as the project sponsor (the person who's requested the project – usually the one who is paying for it) and 'champions' who can support and promote the different areas of the work.

Control

As soon as authorization is received to start work, the project manager must plan the route of the project, assess what risks are involved, identify what skills and resources are required, then constantly check progress and adjust the project's course to make sure the targets are achieved successfully.

Step three:
Know what skills are required

The project manager is often seen as a juggler, the person who has to keep all the balls in the air at once – plans, budgets, people, communications and so on, as well as maintaining the balance between the three parameters of time, cost and quality (see p. 13). Project managers therefore need to have a good level of know-how in whatever field their project is in (such as IT or manufacturing expertise, for example), as well as sufficient 'clout' to have influence with senior decision-makers.

All these requirements can be split into two different areas of skills that the project manager needs: business and interpersonal.

Business

✓ Plan all aspects of the project.

✓ Monitor costs, efficiency and quality without generating unnecessary extra work for others.

✓ Use both technical and general management skills to control the project.

✓ Make sure that the whole team takes part in decision-making, which boosts trust and productivity.

✓ Get things done right the first time without being a slave driver.

✓ Get the right people for the right task at the right time.

✓ See clear-sightedly through tangled issues.

✓ Keep focused on results.

✓ Demonstrate excellent problem-solving skills.

Interpersonal

✓ Lead both by example and by taking a back seat when appropriate.

✔ Negotiate any project requirements (such as suitable timescales and budgets) with senior decision-makers.

✔ Motivate with integrity, sensitivity and imagination.

✔ Build excellent team relationships.

✔ Communicate clearly and unambiguously with everyone involved.

Step four:
Understand the project lifecycle

Any project has a natural progression, from when it is first established to when it is finished and the benefits are seen, moving through a series of different stages. This is known as the project lifecycle.

Depending on their complexity, some projects will need more stages than others. Having said that, the same steps can generally be applied to any sort of objective.

✔ Evaluate ideas

This stage establishes the business need for the project; documents the initial idea(s); assesses the benefits; identifies risks that might threaten the success of the project; and outlines how the project is going to be done, how long it will take, what it will cost and whose authority will be needed to proceed.

✔ Define and design

Now you're into more of the detail. How will you run the project; who will be needed to do it; how will you divide up the responsibilities; and what key measures and milestones will you use to monitor progress? To make sure things don't get missed out, think about it in terms of what your business/team needs, what customers need and what your competitors are up to. Do they have any new initiatives that you need to improve on, for example?

✔ Build and test

With all your plans and designs in place and agreed, you can now find and build all the new processes, places and people involved in the project. At every stage, you should test to make sure that everything works as it's meant to.

✔ Implement, pilot and launch

At this stage, you pilot the project, evaluate how it's gone so far and refine things as necessary. Then you finalize the full-scale launch, prepare the processes and systems that will be required, and make provision for any necessary training. This is the last point at which your project sponsor(s) can make a final decision on whether or not to go ahead.

✔ Evaluate and monitor

Following the launch, you make sure that the project has delivered the expected benefits. You also record any learning points so that you can more effectively manage next time – things are bound to go wrong along the way but if you learn from them, you'll start your next project much better equipped.

TOP TIP

This process won't necessarily flow through in one smooth sequence, as you will need to keep evaluating and monitoring plans, budgets, timescales and so on throughout the life of the project. However, it does act as a good 'road map', and none of the stages should be missed out, even if your project is quite a small one.

Common mistakes

X You don't do enough planning

Once the go-ahead has been given for a new project, it's tempting to get overexcited and rush into a frenzy of activity. All projects stand or fall on how well they've been planned and researched from the outset, though, so the early stages of any project (the 'evaluate ideas' and 'define and design' steps described above) are by far the most important, and it's essential that you place high emphasis on them. In fact, between 30 and 50 per cent of the entire project lifecycle ought to be devoted to investigation before you even think about building or producing any products or processes.

Research has shown clearly that time spent on these stages is valuable in several important ways:

✓ It significantly decreases the time to completion and can cut costs dramatically.

✓ It results in clearer objectives and plans, which are more likely to be achieved.

✓ Since decisions taken at the early stages of a project have a far-reaching effect, it sets the tone for the remainder of the process.

✓ It minimizes the chances of any changes having to be made once development is under way, which can be very costly.

Doing your groundwork properly will greatly lessen the chances of you ending up with a disaster on your hands!

✗ You underestimate the impact of a new project

Because projects, by their very nature, are designed to bring about change, you may meet a lot of resistance from the people potentially affected by them. If you are the project manager, you need to be really sure of what the benefits will be and you also have to be good at getting these across to others. You're also likely to encounter considerable internal politics, with people wanting to influence the process and clashing with each other, so be prepared for that, too.

✗ You get too involved in the nitty-gritty

With so much going on around you, it's all too easy to get distracted by details of each individual activity within a project. It's vital that someone stays in the driving seat and keeps all the activities together and on course, though, and as the project manager, that's your job.

Don't be tempted to get in there and get your hands dirty – you have enough to do already.

BUSINESS ESSENTIALS

✓ Understand the difference between a project and ongoing work.

✓ Recognize that project management is often a way of bringing about change in an organization in a controlled fashion, with minimum disruption to the rest of the business.

✓ If you're in charge, it's important to review your project-management skills, both business and interpersonal, and refresh or update them if necessary.

✓ Move through all the stages of the project lifecycle in order, and don't be tempted to skip any – even if your project is relatively small.

✓ Do lots of groundwork in the early stages of the project. Planning and research will really pay off, even if you're itching to get started on the main job at hand.

✓ Be prepared for the resistance, conflict and internal politics that can result from the changes brought about by a project.

✓ Keep your eye on the big picture, and don't get distracted by detail.

2
Managing your time

The one thing a project manager never has enough of is time. There are so many demands – such as planning and allocating work, monitoring progress, motivating the team, keeping everyone happy, preparing for launch – that time is an extremely precious commodity.

Few people are naturally great at managing their time. With some forethought and discipline, though, it's remarkable how time can be used well and redistributed to encompass everything that needs to be done. This chapter suggests some techniques that, with practice, can result in a calm, productive project manager rather than a harassed individual stretched too thinly in too many different directions!

Step one:
Understand the nature of time

The first thing to remember is that time is finite. We all have a tendency to think it'll stretch – 'there's plenty of time', 'I'll do that later', 'of course you can have five minutes', we all say blithely. We often don't realize, though, that we're frittering away a valuable, non-renewable resource.

The most helpful way to think of time is as a bank balance with a set amount of funds in it. Every time we spend some, we are reducing the total. Obviously, we can't really 'save' time; we can only spend it or 'buy it' by reinvesting it in other activities. Thinking of time in this way can make you much more conscious of how you use it. For example:

- giving it away. Do you realize how much time you give away freely? We rarely hand over money on request (particularly if we know we won't get it back), but if someone asks for time, we'll probably agree happily ... and even ask politely if they want more of it;

- being robbed. People also steal our time. How often do you sit waiting for those who are late for meetings or patiently put up with slow service in a restaurant? If this stealing of hours and minutes were related to money, you'd call the police!

TOP TIP

Learn to use your 'scrap' time productively. Try working on the train or plane, or spend driving hours listening to language tapes, for example. It's amazing how these oddments accumulate, and what you can achieve if you make proper use of them.

Step two:
Work out your time wasters

'Where does the time go?' we mutter to ourselves, as yet another day draws to a close. Well, where does it go? If you look at your daily routine for a week or so, you'll probably see that you waste time in the same ways every day. Once you know the principal eaters of your time, it becomes much easier to reduce or eliminate them, and therefore to become more productive. There's an easy exercise you can do to identify these black holes.

1. Take a sheet of A4 paper and divide it into columns, one for each of your typical daily activities – not forgetting the mundane items such as scheduling meetings or answering emails.

2. Split each column into 15-minute boxes, from the beginning to the end of your working day (8.30 a.m. to 6.00 p.m., for example).

3. Then put crosses in the boxes according to how much time you spent on that activity during the day. If you spend an hour in a meeting, for instance, that column gets four crosses.

4. Total up the used time under each heading at the end of the day, and then again at the end of a week.

You'll probably be horrified to learn exactly how much time you spend chatting at the coffee machine, compared to the time you have spent on important report writing!

TOP TIP

Once you've identified where your time goes, ask yourself these four essential questions:

1. What should I stop doing?

2. What should I be more aware of?

3. What am I spending too much time on?

4. What should I spend more time on?

Step three:
Take control

Most people's trouble with time management stems from the fact that they are always reactive. Unexpected things happen – you react; urgent tasks need doing – you react; people interrupt you – you react. You're always rushing to keep up with external events that you have no control over.

However, you need to learn how to become the opposite: proactive. This means that you decide what needs doing and when; you decide how much time you will allocate to each task; you choose when it is appropriate to deal with other people, and you allocate time to deal with unexpected events. In other words, you take the initiative and, in doing so, gain the control that will let you plan and organize your own time and help your team make the best use of theirs.

There are four main ways of achieving this:

● prioritizing tasks;

● planning what gets done and when;

- knowing what not to do;
- eliminating or minimizing interruptions and external time wasters.

Read on for all you need to know about each!

Step four:
Know how to prioritize

First things first: in order to prioritize how you use your time, you need to know how to distinguish between what is important and what is urgent. Appreciating the full meaning of each is key.

Important activities are highly strategic and will make the most difference in whether or not your project succeeds in the long term.

Urgent activities, on the other hand, normally have to be tackled immediately, though they don't automatically relate to a critical issue for your project. For example, your car could be causing an obstruction outside the office. Urgent? Yes. Important to the work in hand? No.

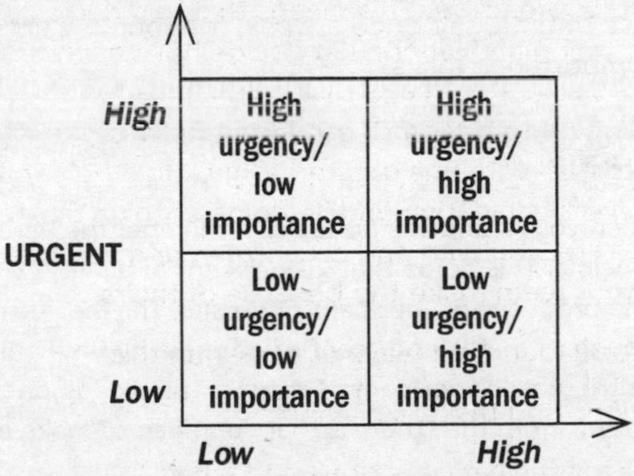

	Low importance	High importance
High	High urgency/ low importance	High urgency/ high importance
Low	Low urgency/ low importance	Low urgency/ high importance

URGENT (vertical axis), Low — High (horizontal axis)

The best way to prioritize tasks is to split everything that needs doing into four categories, as shown in the diagram above – then deal with them as follows:

- low urgency/low importance: Put it on a to-do list (see pp. 29–30);

- low urgency/high importance: Put it in your diary, but DO get it done soon. This is the category that is likely to achieve the most long-term gains;

- high urgency/low importance: Delegate it;

- high urgency/high importance: Do it yourself, NOW!

The general rule is to start with your most important tasks and tackle them one by one, making sure that you finish each before starting the next. Don't try to get the easy things out of the way first, or you might find yourself looking back and wondering where the day went, without even starting the most important job.

'But what if I never manage to get the routine stuff done?', you may ask. The secret is to allocate yourself a block of time, say once a week, for your low urgency/high importance tasks.

TOP TIP

When you're prioritizing tasks, remember the Pareto Principle. This holds that 20 per cent of quality time produces 80 per cent of results. The flipside, though, is that 80 per cent of non-quality time only contributes 20 per cent of results. The big lesson to draw from this, then, is that you need to make as much of your time as possible quality time, as clearly this is the most productive. It's just as important to identify the tasks that will yield the most significant results – don't be one of those people who spends 80 per cent of their time just keeping busy!

Step five:
Make proper plans

Once you've decided on your priorities, you can plan how to organize your time. We talk in Chapter 5 about normal project planning, but personal time planning is just as important.

An excellent way to do this is to use a combination of a 'to-do list' and a diary (calendar/planner/organizer):

- your to-do list is the master list for all the activities you and your team need to accomplish, and it is ongoing. Every time something else crops up that needs to be done, it gets added to the to-do list;

- your diary (calendar/planner/organizer) is where you put any tasks of strategic importance, with blocks of time allocated to them, to make sure they get done.

So, at the beginning of each week:

✓ Set aside 10 minutes and work out everything you and your team need to get done.

✓ List all tasks on your to-do list.

✓ Prioritize them as discussed on pp. 27–28.

✓ Put the top priority/most important strategic tasks in your diary and allocate an appropriate amount of time to them.

TOP TIP

There's a golden rule here! Put the important tasks in the diary, and the less important tasks on your to-do list. That way, you will always have time allocated for your most important jobs, but needn't worry if your to-do list isn't all finished.

The to-do list time trap

Never simply use a to-do list on its own – it contains an in-built time trap. What happens is that you add every single thing that needs doing on it and feel very pleased with yourself and organized. But then, because there's no order or prioritization to it, it's far too easy to spend time doing the smaller, easier tasks.

You'll certainly end up with a nice number of 'ticks' on your list, but it may well be at the expense of more complex jobs that are actually much more important overall.

Useful tips for diary planning

✔ Don't arrange meetings first thing in the morning. Most people are at their highest level of productivity early in the day, so use this time for your important work.

✔ If possible, block out the first two hours of the workday for yourself, and put it in your diary (paper or electronic). You can then get the most important work done before the inevitable fires flare up.

✓ Always factor in a little extra time to deal with any unexpected problems that might crop up.

✓ If you have something important to do, book an appointment with yourself in the diary, tell everyone that's what you're doing, then shut your office door (if you have one), set your phone to voicemail, put a notification on your email, and press on with it.

TOP TIP

Remember Parkinson's Law: 'Work expands to fill the time available for its completion.' In other words, if you allocate a day to clean your house, it'll normally take at least a day, if not slightly longer. Yet if you only had an hour before guests were due, the chances are that you'd do most of it in that time! The lesson is, while the time allocated to achieve a particular goal must be reasonable, don't make it too long ... it'll take all the time you give it.

Step six:
Deal with distractions

The hardest part of any job is getting started, so the last thing you need, once you're motivated to get going, is to be interrupted. In Step two, we covered the ways in which you waste your own time and identified time wasters. You need to be just as disciplined when you're dealing with external distractions.

Here are a few ideas on how to deflect things that might wreck your momentum.

✓ Choose unusual times for people to come back and see you in person, or phone you. For example, get the person who's asking for five minutes of your time to return at 10.35 on the dot. If the matter is that important, she or he will be back on time. If not, they won't come back, or they'll be late – in which case you can rebook them, given that you've probably gone on to something else.

✓ Close your office door (if you have one) so people think twice about entering.

✓ If you have an assistant, divert your phone or email to them for set hours each day, and then return calls or messages in batches. Alternatively, set a voicemail and email notification that you are unavailable for a specific time.

✓ Encourage others to think for themselves. Sometimes people forget that they can take the initiative and may defer to you too much. Ask the other person what they think the answer to the question at hand is, and then take it from there. Guide them if necessary and if they come up with the right answer themselves, so much the better.

TOP TIP

Deferring interruptions until later is a great test of how important they are. You'll find that most are really simply urgent (rather than urgent and important) and they'll get resolved successfully in another way.

Common mistakes

✗ You don't delegate

It's tempting to do something routine yourself, rather than briefing someone else to do it. Similarly, it's easy to set about doing trivial work for the pure satisfaction of feeling busy and achieving lots of ticks on your to-do list. However, it's almost certain that your time could be much better spent on important project tasks. Delegation is always worth the effort, and being disciplined about doing it will make sure that you don't overcommit by trying to be everywhere at once.

✗ You can't say no

Being too thoughtful and taking on too much can cripple any well-meaning project manager. Having the courage to say 'no' is your first line of defence. The way you do that is, of course, important: you need to be firm, but there's no point in being aggressive. You'll get much better results if you stick to your guns but keep positive, friendly and upbeat.

✗ You work in a mess

It's staggering how important order is for general personal effectiveness. Research has shown that people lose hours looking for things that have been mislaid or mis-filed – spreadsheets, bills, document files, contact details, a notebook or stapler, and so on. A tidy (or at least organized) work environment, both physical and digital, is very important: clutter creates confusion, is extremely frustrating and wastes huge amounts of time.

BUSINESS ESSENTIALS

✓ Understand that time is a precious, finite resource, and can be spent, wasted and stolen in the same way as money.

✓ Work out where your time goes each day, and identify the principal time wasters.

✓ Become proactive instead of reactive, and control events rather than letting them control you.

✓ Learn to distinguish between urgent and important, and use these categories to help you to prioritize tasks.

✓ Plan effectively, using a combination of to-do lists and your diary (calendar/organizer) to ensure important tasks don't get neglected or delayed.

✓ Be disciplined about how you deal with any external interruptions.

✓ Make sure you delegate properly. Be clear about what you want to be done, who's responsible and what the deadline is.

✓ Be assertive, learn to say no and don't take on too much work.

✓ Organize your work environment so you don't become mired in clutter.

3
Building a project team

Most projects require a wide variety of skills to complete the work involved, so with any project you manage, you're likely to have to deal with a whole group of people from different backgrounds. They may be drawn from different parts of your organization or else they may come from a number of separate organizations. Teams made up of people from a range of departments or organizations are often called 'cross-functional teams'.

Whichever's the case, it's the project manager's job to bring them together and form them into an effective team that operates as one to achieve the overall goals of the project. Unsurprisingly, this can sometimes be tricky. However, there are a number of rules which, if followed, can make team building much easier and more likely to succeed. This chapter lays out the basics.

Step one:
Identify the skills you require

Start off by identifying and engaging a team of people with the right skills and enthusiasm for the project. This list, obviously, will vary enormously depending on the size of your project and what it entails. Say, for example, you are organizing an office move: you're likely to need floor planners, packers, removal men, electricians to do the wiring, IT people to sort out the computers and so on.

Your team will probably need to come from all parts of your company, so that you bring together people with the right skills and also so that you get input and involvement from all parts of the business. You may well find that your senior stakeholder (the senior manager who has agreed to the project idea, for example; see Chapter 4 for more help on building a great relationship with stakeholders) can help you find and recruit the right people.

Step two:
Get the right mix of personalities

Besides the different skills, it's also worth keeping an eye on the mix of personalities among your team members, as this can have a huge effect on whether the team functions properly or not.

Meredith Belbin, the business writer and academic, identified around a dozen common team roles as part of his research in the 1970s:

BUSINESS ESSENTIALS

Role and characteristic	Function
Leader – aims to get the best out of everyone	Forms the team; sets objectives; monitors performance; provides structure.
Challenger – rocks the boat	Adopts unconventional approaches; challenges the accepted order; comes up with ideas.
Expert – provides specialist advice	Provides a professional viewpoint, often from an external source (e.g. IT, accountancy).
Ambassador – makes friends easily	Develops external relationships; understands external environment; sells the team.
Judge – down to earth, logical, careful	Listens; evaluates; ponders before deciding; avoids arguments; seeks truth and the best way.
Innovator – provides source of vision, ingenuity and creativity	Uses imagination; motivates others; evaluates, builds and provides creativity on ideas; deals with complex issues.
Diplomat – steers team to successful outcome	Influential; builds alliances in and out of the team; good negotiator; aids agreement; often becomes the leader in difficult times.
Conformer – helpful, reliable, co-operative	Fills gaps; jack of all trades; seldom challenges authority.
Outputter – chases progress	Self-motivated; focuses on tasks and results; imposes timescales; checks progress; intolerant of other people.
Supporter/mediator – focuses on team relationships	Builds morale; resolves conflict; gives advice; supports and encourages.
Quality controller – ensures tasks are done well	Checks output; preoccupied with high standards; focuses on quality.
Reviewer – monitors performance	Observes; reviews performance; promotes feedback; looks for pitfalls.

Ideally, you need a good mix of these types of people in your team (bearing in mind that individuals can fulfil more than one role at a time), as you're likely to have problems if you have too many of one type. Imagine a team full of judges, or challengers, for instance!

> **TOP TIP**
>
> Don't worry if your team does contain quite a few of the same type of people – there will be ways around it. For example, you could split your team into smaller 'working parties', each of which is responsible for particular tasks that together contribute to the overall goals.

Step three:
Understand the stages of team formation

Teams go through a number of stages after they are first brought together, and these stages can be responsible for different kinds of problems or issues that arise.

Say, for example, your team is going through a sticky patch and you're having to deal with conflict and arguments. If, rather than wondering what on earth is going wrong, you recognize that this may simply be a result of the stage your team has reached, it will help you judge objectively what – if anything – needs to be done about it.

The four stages are:

1. Forming – excitement is high; everything is new and fun; no one knows what they're doing yet.

2. Storming – roles are assigned; personalities begin to show; uncertainty of others and their abilities can lead to conflict, which can smoulder unless tackled promptly; people don't yet feel safe to be open and honest.

3. Norming – confidence starts to improve; relationships strengthen; differences of opinion are respected; solutions begin to develop; goals become manageable, and everyone starts to work together to achieve them.

4. Performing – the team becomes fluid, with people taking it in turns to lead; delegation occurs so team members grow and flourish; goals and targets are reached regularly and effectively.

Step four:
Help the 'norming' process along

In any team, it is important that the 'vectors' are aligned. A vector is a force that pulls in a certain direction and every project team member will have their own, created by their individual beliefs, thoughts and desires. Within a team, it can be disastrous if everyone's vectors are all straining in different directions – and even one 'anti-vector' or team member forcing the current a separate way can have an adverse effect.

In your role as a project manager, it's your responsibility to get every team member pulling in the same direction to achieve the project goals – a process known as 'vectorship'. Although this sounds obvious, it's extraordinary how many projects fail because individuals who are being negative are allowed to go unchallenged!

The best way to get these vectors aligned is to create a working climate in which mistakes and failures are viewed as learning experiences, not occasions for blame, and where every member feels included 'in the loop'. There are a number of elements that contribute to this type of an atmosphere:

- A free flow of information. Make sure that every member receives/has easy access to any information they need to do their job.

- Open communication. Don't keep secrets, or allow team members to feel that some people are privy to information and others aren't.

- Frequent feedback. People need to know how well they're doing – and if and where improvements can be made.

- Regular one-to-one interaction. Talk to your team members as people, and use the time to make sure they're happy and on side.

- A listening culture. Make sure that people feel free to say what they think without fear or anger, and that they will be heard, even when they're voicing minority or unpopular views.

Step five:
Learn what motivates people

Motivation is essential for individuals and teams to work effectively and harmoniously. Studies into what motivates people at work have revealed that motivators and demotivators are not necessarily the same thing. In other words, the things that make people feel motivated and enthusiastic are not always the same things that, if unsatisfactory, make them feel discontented and apathetic.

The table below identifies the top 10 motivators for project team members, and the top 10 demotivators*:

Motivators	Score	Demotivators	Score
Recognition	1	Relations with project manager	1
Achievement	2	Team peer relations	2
Responsibility	3	Salary	3
Team peer relations	4	Project manager's leadership	4
Salary	5	Security	5
Relations with project manager	6	Work conditions	6
Project manager's leadership	7	Organization's policy	7
Work itself	8	Team subordinate relations	8
Advancement	9	Personal time	9
Personal growth	10	Title/status	10

* Yourzak, R. J. 'Motivation in the Project Environment', *Field Guide to Project Management*. New Jersey: John Wiley & Sons, 2004

These lists prove the point: some things, if they're good, are hardly noticed – but they cause high levels of dissatisfaction if they're bad.

TOP TIP

Go through your list of team members and consider what you think might motivate each of them, or small groups of them if this is more appropriate. Then consider whether any of the demotivators listed in the table on p. 41 are present in your project or organization.

Is there anything you can do to boost the positives and minimize the effect of the negatives?

Step six:
Delegate

Delegation is another vital tool for managing your team effectively. It's not something that everyone finds easy to start with, but it does get easier with practice and will help your project run smoothly. Here are the basic rules:

- ✓ Select the most appropriate person for the task. Depending on what the job is, you might not have to always delegate downwards, to your team: you can also delegate upwards (to your manager) or sideways (to a peer).

- ✓ Communicate clearly to whomever will be helping you, so that he or she is certain about what they should be coming back to you with, and when.

- ✓ Break down tasks into manageable chunks, probably with deadlines at each stage when the other person can report back and let you know that things are moving in the right direction.

✓ Keep proper records so you know what tasks you are delegating and to whom.

Here's a quick summary of how much supervision is needed, depending on a person's previous experience and their motivation:

1. New or inexperienced person, low confidence:
   ✓ Tell the person what to do.

   ✓ Show them how to do it.

   ✓ Put a plan together, showing each checkpoint when they have to report back to you.

   ✓ Review the task and give feedback.

2. Slightly more experience/confidence:
   Tell the person what your desired outcome is, and plan the steps together. Less frequent checkpoints than 1.

3. More experienced, though needs some guidance and help:
   Tell the person what your desired outcome is and allow them to plan it, and establish when checkpoints are necessary.

4. Experienced, committed person:
   Explain the required outcome, timescales and checkpoints (if any), and leave them to get on with it. But don't abdicate all responsibility for a task; you are the project leader and are ultimately responsible for everything!

TOP TIP

The secret of good delegation (and supervision) is to put yourself into your team members' shoes. Imagine being a really capable professional who knows and enjoys what you're doing, but having a project manager who's constantly peering over your shoulder and commenting on how you do your job! Conversely, think what it would be like for a new recruit, who's still very unsure of themselves and their role, to be managed by a 'hands-off' boss who simply leaves them to sink or swim. How would you react under those circumstances?

Step seven:
Resolve conflict

Projects can be breeding grounds for conflict because they are temporary situations and circumstances within them tend to change continually. Unresolved conflict can be very destructive, so it needs to be tackled immediately. Here's how.

Recognize conflict

Conflict can be either overt (clearly visible and stemming from an easily identifiable cause), or covert (bubbling under the surface, from a less obvious or apparently unrelated cause).

Monitor the climate

Look out for early warning signals so that you can deal with the conflict quickly, before it gets out of hand. Early action saves time and stress later.

Research the situation

Spend time finding out the true root cause of the
conflict, who is involved and what the potential effects
are. Putting yourself in other people's shoes will enable
you to understand and empathize better.

Plan your approach

Encourage everyone involved to be open and
understanding in the way they interact with others.
It might be a good idea to ask people to write down
their thoughts and feelings, so that they can express
themselves logically and constructively.

Tackle the issue

✓ Give everyone an opportunity to express their point
  of view.

✓ Avoid fight or flight: fighting back will only make
  the situation worse, while running away from
  the situation will show that you don't feel up to
  resolving the situation, and may lead to a loss of
  respect for you.

✓ Remember to be assertive. Becoming aggressive
  will get you nowhere, but being passive won't
  achieve anything either.

✓ Acknowledge the views and rights of all parties.

✓ Encourage those involved to come up with their
  own solution – if they've created the solution, they
  are more likely to buy into it.

✓ Suggest a constructive way forwards.

Common mistakes

✗ You don't involve your team early enough in decision-making

Making too many rules and trying to impose your own plans and methods on your team without getting their input is just asking for trouble. You've brought these people together for their skills – so involve them from the start. Not only will they provide a fresh perspective, information and ideas, but they also will feel as if they 'own' the plans, all of which boost their level of commitment.

This doesn't, however, mean that your projects should be planned by committee, rather than you; as manager, plan the project based on all the available experience and creative ideas. Perhaps you could attempt the first level(s) of planning to help explain the project to the team and then ask for comments. Then, using these, allocate the final breakdown of tasks to the people who'll actually be carrying them out.

✗ You micromanage

Don't go there! You'll explode with the effort of trying to oversee every detail yourself, and your team will quickly lose motivation. Delegate the work and supervise it appropriately, but do keep your eye mainly on the overall direction of the project – the 'big picture'. As project manager, that's your job!

BUSINESS ESSENTIALS

✓ Identify the skills that are needed to make the project happen, and then find the people with those skills.

✓ Remember that a great team is made up of a mix of different personalities. Don't just recruit people like you, either.

✓ Understand the different stages of team formation. You'll need to take the rough with the smooth and not panic.

✓ Create a good climate in which the team can function effectively.

✓ Don't shut yourself away in your office: talk to your team regularly.

✓ Remember that different people understand in different ways, and adjust how you present information accordingly.

✓ Recognize what factors motivate (and demotivate) people.

✓ Don't be afraid to delegate!

✓ Spot conflict as early as possible, and take immediate steps to resolve it.

✓ Involve team members in project decisions right from the start.

✓ Keep your eye on the big picture.

4
Working with a project sponsor and stakeholders

It's all too easy, when you're working on a project, to become so involved with your team and the work in hand that you overlook a very important group of people. These are your sponsor and stakeholders – in other words, all those who may have an investment or interest in the project's outcome without being directly involved in making it happen.

Neglect them at your peril! This group is likely to have opinions and influences that can make all the difference to the success or failure of the whole project. The wise project manager will make sure that he or she knows from the outset who all these people are, what form their interest in the project takes and their needs and desires, and will then work out how to start and maintain a great working relationship with them. This chapter shows you how.

Step one:
Understand what a 'sponsor' and a 'stakeholder' are

✓ The project sponsor is the individual or organization for whom the project is undertaken – the primary risk-taker, in other words. This usually means the person or body responsible for financing the project. The project sponsor is far and away your most important stakeholder.

✓ Stakeholders are people who are not directly involved in the project but are affected by it in some way, and so have a vested interest in its successful or unsuccessful conclusion. As a result, they (and their views) must be taken into account by the project manager and the sponsor. The most common type of stakeholder is the user – that is, the group of people who will be using the end product – but they can also include people such as your boss, suppliers, customers and even your family.

Step two:
Know why it's essential to have these people 'on side'

There are a number of important benefits to having a really good relationship with your sponsor and stakeholders.

✓ If you consult the most powerful among them early on, you can use their opinions to shape your project from the outset. Not only does this make it more likely that they will support you, but their input can also improve the quality of your work (and stop you having to do things twice).

✓ Gaining support from powerful stakeholders can also help you to win valuable additional resources – which also means that your project will be more likely to succeed.

✓ If you keep in touch regularly with stakeholders, you'll know that they fully understand what you're doing and what the benefits are. As a result, they'll feel more involved and will probably be willing to support you actively when necessary.

✓ Through stakeholders, you can anticipate what other's reactions to your project may be and build in plans that will win widespread support.

✓ Good stakeholder management also helps you to deal with the politics that can often come with major projects, and thus eliminate a potential source of stress.

TOP TIP

Remember that your sponsor, having the biggest interest in your project, is not a 'silent partner' and does have the right to make decisions. If you think these are wrong, be honest about what you think (but don't be confrontational). If, after all that, the sponsor still wants it done his or her way, follow instructions and do your best to make sure the outcome is successful.

Step three:
Work out exactly who your stakeholders are

It will be perfectly obvious who most of your stakeholders are, but there may well be a few who don't come to mind immediately. It's a good idea to have a brainstorming session with your project team to make sure no one gets left out of the loop. Think about all the people who are affected by your work, who have power or influence over it or who have an interest in whether it succeeds or fails.

The table below shows some of the people who might be stakeholders in projects:

Your boss	Your project sponsor	Government
Senior executives	Business partners	Trades associations
Your colleagues	Suppliers	The press
Your team	Lenders	Interest groups
Customers	Analysts	The public
Prospective customers	Future recruits	The community
Your family	Trade unions	Shareholders

TOP TIP

Remember that although stakeholders may be both organizations and people, at the end of the day you communicate with people, not buildings. Make sure, then, that you have a contact at any stakeholder organization with whom you can then build a good relationship.

Step four:
Analyze who takes priority

If you write down all the people who might fit into the categories above, as well as anyone else you can think of who will be affected by your project, you may well end up with quite a long list. You don't have enough time to deal with them all equally, so how do you decide who takes precedence?

The best option is to categorize them by their power over your work and their interest in your work, as shown in the grid below.

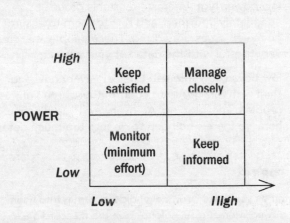

Go through the list of people you've identified as your stakeholders, and write their names in the section that seems most appropriate. For example, your boss is likely to have high power over your project and high interest, and will therefore go in the top right-hand corner of the grid. Your family may have high interest but are unlikely to have power over it (so they'll be in the bottom right-hand corner). Someone's position on the grid shows you how you ought to deal with them:

- high power/high interest: These are the people you must make the greatest efforts to satisfy, so make sure you communicate with them very regularly and get them on side;

- high power/low interest: Put in enough work to keep them satisfied, but not so much that they get bored with your message;

- low power/high interest: Keep this group adequately informed, and talk to them to ensure no major issues are arising. These people are often very helpful with the detail of your project;

- low power/low interest: Check in every now and then with this group to confirm there aren't any problems developing. An overview is usually fine here, so there's no need to go into too much detail!

TOP TIP

When you write your stakeholders' names into your power/interest grid, colour-code them according to whether they're likely to support you or to be opposed to your project. Strong advocates could be written in green; more neutral people could be in orange; and serious critics could be in red ... for danger! Red-alert people in the high-power quadrant will need particularly careful management.

Step five:
Understand your key stakeholders

So now you know who they are and what sort of priority they should have for your attention, you need to know more about your stakeholders themselves; in particular, how they are likely to feel about and react to your project, and how best to engage and communicate with them.

Key questions that can help you understand your stakeholders are:

- What financial or emotional interest do the stakeholders have in the outcome of your work? Is it positive or negative?

- What motivates them most of all?

- What information do they want from you?

- How do they want to receive information from you?

- What is the best way of communicating your message to them?

- What is their current opinion of your work? Is it based on good information?

- Who influences their opinions generally? Do some of these influencers therefore become important stakeholders in their own right?

- If they're not likely to be positive, what will win them round to support your project?

- If you don't think you will be able to win them round, how will you manage their opposition?

- Who else might be influenced by their opinions?

The best way to answer these questions is to talk to your stakeholders directly. People are usually quite open about their views, and asking their opinions is often the first step in building a successful relationship with them – they'll be pleased that their views are being taken into account.

Step six:
Plan how you'll communicate with your stakeholders

The next step is to draw up a communications plan, so that you can make sure the right messages get to the right people in the right format.

TOP TIP

Communication is vital: there's always a danger that while a project is in progress, the project team slogs away and takes the attitude that 'everyone should leave us alone until we've finished, and then we'll deliver a wonderful product'.

Stakeholders who are keen to see a successful result can become nervous if they have no indication of how things are progressing, so you must keep in touch with them.

There are eight different aspects that you need to consider while drawing up your plan. These are:

1. Stakeholders
    Who are you trying to reach (you'll know this from your initial brainstorming session)?

2. Objectives
   What are the objectives of the communication?
   Is it to prompt action, gain approval or merely
   to inform?

3. Message
   What are the key messages you want to
   get across? These should be targeted at the
   individual stakeholders according to their
   influence and interest. Typical messages will
   show the benefits to the person or organization
   of what you are doing and will focus on key
   issues, such as increasing profitability or
   delivering real improvements.

4. Information
   What information will you communicate? There
   may be issues of confidentiality that must be
   carefully addressed.

5. Channel
   What channels will you use? The choice of
   channel for a particular stakeholder will depend
   upon the Message, Feedback, Level and
   Timing aspects, not to mention geography (i.e.
   where they are located relative to you). You
   probably have a multitude of choices available
   to you – meetings, video-conferencing, email,
   newsletters, telephone, workshops and press
   conferences, for example.

6. Feedback
   How will you encourage feedback, and
   what mechanisms should you have in place
   to respond to it? For example, you could
   have a dedicated email address for queries,

which a member of your project team is
responsible for.

7. Level
   How much detail should be provided?

8. Timing
   When should you communicate? It's no good
   leaving it until the end and then telling everyone
   that the project is finished!

The simplest way to organize all this information into
an easy-to-follow communications plan is to plot it into
a table of some kind.

Say, for example, your project is to construct a new
social space for the local community, and you've
decided your main forms of communication will be:
consultation meetings during design; monthly site
meetings; monthly progress presentations; a page in
local media; and an open day. You could set them out
as shown in the table below.

Stakeholder	Consultation meetings	Site meetings	Progress presentation	Press and/ or social media	Open day
Councillors	✔		✔		✔
Project sponsor	✔	✔	✔		✔
Architect	✔	✔			✔
Builder	✔			✔	
Residents			✔	✔	

Stakeholder	Consultation meetings	Site meetings	Progress presentation	Press and/ or social media	Open day
Facilities manager	✔	✔	✔		✔
Local authority	✔		✔		✔

You can use simple tables of this type to illustrate various aspects of the communications plan. Keep the stakeholders down the left-hand side and change the column headings as you need to – they could relate to timings, information, message, channel and so on. There are no set rules: just use whichever layout is most appropriate for your project.

TOP TIP

Flag up potential problems as early as you can. This gives everyone time to think through how to move forwards, and also preserves your reputation for reliability. No one will be happy to be told at the last minute that a project is not going to be delivered on time or to budget.

Common mistakes

✗ You go over the top

It's just as damaging to relations with stakeholders to go over the top as to provide too little information. The company chairman is not going to be amused to receive every detail of every quote you get in for materials and supplies! Be sensible about judging the level of detail you give to whom, and how much time you spend on managing your stakeholders; it all depends on the size and complexity of your projects and goals, and the time you have available.

✗ You don't consider what you want from each individual or group

Stakeholders are likely to be a disparate lot, and you'll probably need very different kinds of support from each of them. Your family, you hope, will be understanding about you working at weekends (if necessary); your boss, you'd also hope, will be understanding about you not giving priority to his or her immediate work. You'll need to communicate with each stakeholder or group of stakeholders in very different ways: there's no point bombarding them all with the same progress presentations if they're just not suitable for everyone.

BUSINESS ESSENTIALS

✓ Understand why it's essential to have your project sponsor and stakeholders on your side. They have the power to make your project succeed or fail.

✓ Brainstorm exactly who they all are, so no one gets left out of the loop.

✓ Work out who takes priority according to their power over, or interest in, your project.

✓ Understand what motivates each stakeholder or group of stakeholders, and what actions might win their support (if you don't have it already).

✓ Come up with a comprehensive communications plan that's tailored to suit the needs of your various audiences.

5
Planning, scheduling and budgeting

Estimation – whether it be in connection with plans, budgets or schedules – is one of the darker arts of project management. This is because there are always so many unknowns: details that might change, issues that might arise or events that might derail the best-laid plans. However, it is also among the most important skills for the project manager and plays a key role in a project's success.

There are many tools and techniques you can use to overcome the problems of uncertainty, and in this chapter, we'll be looking at the main ones.

Step one:
Know your planning tools

Drawing up a detailed project plan is your most vital ingredient for a successful, pain-free project. The tools you use to do this will obviously depend greatly on what you're doing – the size of your project, its complexity and deadline, for example – but here are some of the most useful ones.

Work breakdown structure

This is useful for identifying the individual tasks that must be performed in your project.

✓ Get the team together and brainstorm all the tasks that need doing, in no particular order.

✓ Write them down on sticky notes and put them up on a board or wall.

✓ Once everyone has thought of as many tasks as they can, arrange the sticky notes into groups under the major areas of activity.

Project logic diagram

Next, put start and end sticky notes at opposite ends of the board or wall.

✓ From left to right between them, arrange the sticky notes in the logical sequence of activities.

✓ Join the notes with arrows in and out, depending on whether things can be done one after another or at the same time (some tasks may have more than one arrow).

✓ Under each task, write how long you estimate that it will take.

You have now created a 'project logic diagram', which should help you identify which tasks are dependent and which ones are parallel.

Dependent tasks: Some activities are dependent on others being completed first. For example, it is not a good idea to start building a bridge before you have designed it or arranged financing! These dependent activities need to be completed in a sequence, with each stage being more or less completed before the next can begin.

Parallel tasks: These are the tasks that are not dependent on the completion of anything else and may be done at any time before or after a particular stage is reached.

You can then put these tasks into a simple timetable or action plan, or use either of the next two planning tools to create a more formal structure for how the work should proceed.

Gantt charts

A very popular tool, Gantt charts are most useful for analyzing and planning small or medium-sized projects. They:

- help you plan the tasks involved;
- give a basis for scheduling when tasks will be carried out;
- allow you to allocate the necessary resources;
- help plot the critical path for a project that must be completed by a particular date.

To produce a Gantt chart, take all the activities for the project that you listed in your project logic diagram and, for each task, show the earliest start date, estimated time it will take, whether it is parallel or dependent and, if dependent, which other tasks it depends on.

Let's say your project is to manage an office move. Your task list might look like this:

Task	Earliest start date	Length	Type
1. Produce a new floor plan	Day 1	2 days	
2. Pack up current office	Day 3	1 day	Dependent on 1.
3. Organize facilities	Day 3	1 day	Parallel.
4. Transport furniture	Day 4	2 days	Dependent on 2.
5. Transport equipment	Day 5	2 days	Parallel, dependent on 4. Any time after.
6. Unpack in new office	Day 6	3 days	Parallel, dependent on 4. Any time after.
7. Set up IT systems	Day 7	4 days	Parallel, dependent on 5. Any time after.
8. Staff move in	Day 10	2 days	Parallel, dependent on 7. Any time after.

You can plot the list into a chart, like the one below:

	1	2	3	4	5	6	7	8	9	10	11
Task	Mon	Tues	Wed	Thur	Fri	Sun	Mon	Tues	Wed	Thur	Fri
1. Produce a new floor plan		♦									
2. Pack up current office											

	1	2	3	4	5	6	7	8	9	10	11
Task	Mon	Tues	Wed	Thur	Fri	Sun	Mon	Tues	Wed	Thur	Fri
3. Organize new facilities (lighting, phones, etc.)											
4. Transport furniture											
5. Transport equipment											
6. Unpack in new office								◆			
7. Set up IT systems										◆	
8. Staff move in											

◆ The diamond shapes are the important 'milestones' or goals that are set to be achieved at different stages of the project.

Once you've plotted your chart, you can see if any adjustments are required. Once the project is under way, the chart will be very useful for monitoring progress, as you can see immediately what should have been achieved at a point in time – and take remedial action if things are slipping.

Critical path analysis

Critical path analysis (CPA) is a powerful tool for scheduling and managing complex projects. The main benefit is that you can use it to identify the tasks that have to be done on time and in sequence in order for the whole project to be completed (the critical path itself). Then you can fit the other non-dependent tasks around them.

Say your project is to launch a new product, and you've listed the tasks as follows:

Task	Type
A Prepare initial designs	
B Make prototypes	Dependent on A.
C Test prototypes	Dependent on B.
D Finalize design	Dependent on C.
E Set up production line	Parallel, dependent on A. Any time after.
F Train operators	Parallel, dependent on E. Any time after.
G Produce first batch	Dependent on D and F.

The diagram below shows how the dependent tasks follow on sequentially from one another, while the parallel tasks are fitted round them to save time.

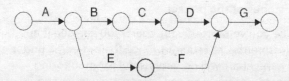

In order to work out the critical path from a network diagram like this, you need to work out which tasks are critical. A task is said to be critical if its duration cannot be extended without delaying the completion of the project.

Looking at the diagram below, you can see that there are three possible paths you could take to get from one side of it to the other. The 'lengths' can be any amount of time you see fit, such as days, weeks or months. Here, we'll assume they're days:

- A–C, with a length of 6 (days);
- B–D, with a length of 7 (days);
- A–D, with a length of 8 (days).

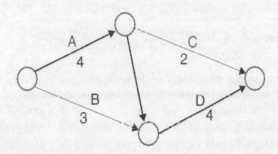

The longest path through a network is called a critical path, and the critical path on this diagram is picked out in bold.

The duration of the project is determined by the longest path, which in this case is A–D. The critical activities are those that lie on the longest path through the network – so here, obviously, A and D are critical.

Any extension or delay in a critical activity will make such a path longer still, thereby delaying completion of the project.

TOP TIP

It's important to remember that complex planning tools aren't always appropriate. If your project is a relatively simple one, a straightforward timetable or action plan might be enough. Over-complicated planning can lead to poor communication and muddled projects. For simple tasks, MS Office 365 subscribers can access the Microsoft Planner, which is similar to Trello. Monday.com, Wrike, Asana, ClickUp and Smartsheet are more sophisticated software options.

Step two:
Allow enough time!

As a rule, people vastly underestimate the amount of time needed to make a project happen, particularly if they're not familiar with the individual tasks to be carried out. They forget to consider unexpected events or unscheduled high-priority work, and they also often simply fail to allow for the full complexity involved with a job. Many people are naturally over-optimistic, so it's all too easy to fall into this particular trap.

However, it's important to get time estimation as accurate as possible for two main reasons:

- you'll save yourself and your team a huge amount of stress;

- you could save yourself a lot of money: if you get your timings wrong and you have to have work done at very short notice, it's highly likely that you'll have to pay a lot more for it;

Also, you'll enhance your reputation as a great project manager if you can deliver to deadline. If you're in a competitive work environment, or if you want to move up the career ladder, making your project successful will really help.

In Step one, we looked at assigning lengths of time to the different tasks within your project, using the expertise and experience of your team to do so. In addition, there are other factors you need to consider when estimating the overall time for the project as a whole. Again, these will vary dramatically depending on the type of project you're working on, but they could include some or all of the following:

- detailed project planning;
- liaison with other parties;
- external and internal meetings;
- quality assurance and any supporting documentation necessary;
- accidents and emergencies;
- holidays and sickness among essential staff;
- contact with customers;
- breakdowns in equipment;
- missed deliveries by suppliers;
- interruptions;
- quality control rejections.

Any combination of these factors may double (or even more than double) the length of time needed to complete a project.

> **TOP TIP**
>
> All problems are solvable in time, so building in
> plenty of contingency time will give you a head start
> if you need to tackle unexpected hurdles.

Step three:
Count the costs

Costs, like time, are often underestimated. If you get
your time more or less right, though, it's then easier to
be accurate with your costs.

The types of costs you should include in your estimates
and in your project plan are outlined below.

One-off development costs

- staff costs for the project – this is usually the
  biggest expense;

- cost of research undertaken;

- systems development costs, including software/
  hardware purchase or licences;

- office refitting/rewiring;

- pilot costs (staff and materials);

- implementation costs – training, recruitment,
  communication, etc.;

- third-party expertise (e.g. software consultants,
  marketing agency);

- government taxes on any third-party services.

Ongoing operating costs

Direct costs:

- overheads – the general operating costs;
- new stocks of materials resulting from the project;
- new administration – purchasing, accounting, record-keeping, etc.;
- costs incurred before the benefits of the project can be realized.

Indirect costs:

- a proportion of the costs of running your business day to day (e.g. office rental, vehicles and expenses, existing staff's additional duties).

TOP TIP

The earlier on in the project you do your cost estimates, the more likely it is that these will only be 'best guesses'. For this reason, it's essential to allow a significant contingency, so as an absolute minimum add a further 20 per cent to what you think the costs will be. Unfortunately, in most cases actual costs tend to be higher than estimated!

Step four:
Identify the benefits

Wherever possible, try to identify the benefits of your project in financial terms so they can be weighed against the costs.

For example, if your project is to develop a new product or service for your clients, you might estimate that this will bring in extra income of X thousand pounds per annum for your organization. Or if the project is to move offices, you might calculate that the new premises will save the company money in terms of rent, cheaper utilities, better facilities (your own canteen, so you don't have to use outside caterers, for example) and so on.

However, not all benefits can be measured financially, so instead, try to find ways of quantifying them in tangible, measurable terms so the success of the project can be assessed. Any benefits that form critical success factors (see below) should be highlighted, as these may be just as influential in getting decision-makers to approve the project as the purely financial benefits.

What are critical success factors?

These are the factors that define how the achievement of project goals will be judged. They need to be measurable and unambiguous, so there cannot be arguments over what they mean.

For example:

'Relocation of offices must be completed by 15 August 2025' is a good critical success factor as it is very clear.

'Work must be completed to a high level of quality', on the other hand, is not, as there's no definition of what 'high quality' means and this could be interpreted in all sorts of different ways.

Step five:
Refine your estimates as you go along

Regardless of how often you emphasize the fact that forecasts of time and costs are approximate estimates to begin with, there is a continual danger that the words 'approximate' and 'estimates' get forgotten as the figures get communicated through the business, and everyone thinks you have given them the final 'completion date' and 'total cost'!

To avoid this particular headache, keep refining your costs and timescales as you work through the project, and then make sure you keep people up to date. Tell any relevant people – your team, customers or stakeholders, for example – and very clearly, too.

The diagram below shows the stages of the project at which you would be wise to check your estimates, and it gives a rough idea of how the accuracy can improve through the project process. For example, your final time and cost estimates could end up being as much as 50 per cent more or 30 per cent less than you've quoted as your initial ballpark figure.

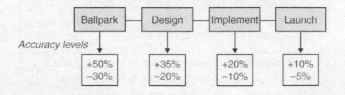

Accuracy levels

Ballpark	Design	Implement	Launch
+50% −30%	+35% −20%	+20% −10%	+10% −5%

Common mistakes

✗ You don't fight to protect your estimates

It doesn't help your accuracy – and therefore your reputation for reliability – if you allow your estimates to be disrupted unnecessarily be external people or circumstances. Once you have arrived at what you consider to be a realistic schedule or budget, fight for it. Never let the outside world deflect you from what you know to be practical. If someone tries to impose a deadline upon you that is impossible, clearly state this and give your reasons.

However, you may need to compromise instead, since a flat 'no' will be seen as obstructive. Look for alternatives, if you can. For example:

✓ Offer a prototype service or product at an earlier date than the end date, on the understanding that your finished project would subsequently replace the prototype.

✓ Reduce the complexity of the product, or the total number of units; future enhancements or more units would then be the subject of a subsequent negotiation.

✓ Demonstrate what other (specified) resources would be required if it's vital that the project is delivered to an earlier deadline.

BUSINESS ESSENTIALS

✓ Plan carefully, using any appropriate tools to help you. Don't overcomplicate the process though – a simple project does not usually require complex planning tools.

✓ Be as accurate as you can regarding timescales, not forgetting to allow for all the extra issues and factors that may arise, apart from the length of time required for the project tasks themselves.

✓ When budgeting, include both the costs that are required to run the project itself, as well as any costs that may arise in your day-to-day running of the project.

✓ As far as possible, quantify the financial benefits of the project, to offset its costs.

✓ Continually refine the accuracy of your estimates throughout the lifecycle of your project.

✓ Once you've set them, defend your estimates as far as possible from unnecessary disruption.

6
Dealing with the unexpected

As we've discussed elsewhere, projects tend to be awkward beasts. Because their whole purpose is to bring about change, they almost always exist in an unsettled and uncertain environment. This inevitably means that unexpected issues tend to crop up – changes are made and mistakes happen. As a project manager, you have to allow for these things and accept that you're never going to eliminate them altogether. The trick is to be prepared for them and to manage them as best you can when they arise.

To keep on top of and lessen the impact of the blips that might come your way, there are some important disciplines you can build into the way you manage your project. This chapter explains what they are and how to use them.

**Step one:
Plan, plan, plan**

Projects do not just happen, they have to be planned. The surest way to make a project fail is to set off without a proper plan – it's like trying to find your way round a strange city without a map!

The plan should be developed by the whole project team, not just the project manager, as this makes sure that everyone's useful experience and expertise is brought together to tackle the tasks right from the beginning. It also means that everyone feels that they've contributed to the project from the start and bought into the overall goals, and that things haven't simply been foisted on them.

A good project plan will provide:

- a 'map' that everyone in the team can follow, with clear milestones along the way;

- a realistic timescale;

- details of what resources are required;

- justification for the estimated costs;

- identification of where tasks might slip;

- early warning of potential problems.

We talked in more detail about scheduling, budgeting and planning tools in Chapter 5, but it's worth remembering that you need to spend time on the early stages of a project. At least 30 to 50 per cent of the entire project lifetime should be devoted to getting the planning right.

Step two:
Manage the risks

Know what a risk is

A risk is something that might happen in the future and which may threaten your success. The sooner a potential risk is identified, the sooner a course of action can be determined to remove or at least minimize it. A risk is assessed on:

- the probability of something happening;
- the impact it would have;
- the action necessary to avoid it.

Identify the risks

When you start to form your ideas about how to tackle the project, do a risk analysis to anticipate any future problems. The first stage of a risk analysis is to identify the kind of risks you may face. Often the best way to do this is to involve all members of the project team in a risk assessment workshop, taking each of the areas in the table below as your agenda. Try to be as thorough as possible when you brainstorm – it can be very easy to overlook potential threats. You may come across the following types of risk:

Risk	What is it?	Questions to ask
Reputational (your brand)	This occurs when a company's image is tarnished by an unpopular action.	• Will it harm perception of your company if you carry out this project (e.g. by your customers/shareholders)? • Does it fit with products/services you already provide?
Operational	This arises if the project requires processes that your business can't support, or it is designed incorrectly through lack of expertise.	• Will any processes incur increased volumes of work or business? If so, can your company cope? • Have new systems been designed for and communicated to the right areas and people? • Might you have to reorganize any area or department of your company?

Risk	What is it?	Questions to ask
People	This could include changes to working conditions or the need to employ new/extra staff.	• Will employees accept changes to working conditions? • If you need extra staff, can the skills easily be found, and can you afford them? • How would you manage if a key person leaves or is ill?
Premises and business continuity	If the project causes a problem with your premises, people or systems, this might threaten your company's whole business.	• Can you operate the project in your existing premises/locations? • If operating the project breaks a key system or process, will this cause your company to cease business (temporarily or permanently)?
Technical	Risks might include advances in technology, technical failure, etc.	• Does the technology you're intending to use fit with what you have already? • Are any new systems sufficiently flexible/scalable?
Financial	Areas include business failure, stock market, unemployment, etc.	• Could any of these spell disaster for your project? • Who would be affected?
Political	These might include changes in tax laws, public opinion, government policy or foreign influence.	• How likely are any of these possibilities? • Would any of them significantly affect the success of your project (e.g. if a foreign exchange rate rose or fell dramatically)?
'Acts of God'	These encompass natural/external events, such as floods, storms, diseases and so on.	• Would your project be adversely affected by any of these (e.g. if it involves building work)? • If so, would changing the timing of the project make a difference (e.g. summer rather than winter)?

TOP TIP

Don't forget that risks to be considered should also include what might happen if you don't do this project. For example, in the project to create a new website, the consequences of not doing so could be far-reaching, with a lack of online presence and visibility for your business likely affecting sales, marketing, customer experience and ultimately profitability.

Evaluate the risk

Once you've identified any possible risks, you need to assess the probability or likelihood of each one happening as:

- high – very likely;
- medium – possible;
- low – unlikely.

Assess the impact in a similar way:

- high – significant threat to your whole company;
- medium – will threaten business;
- low – minor impact only.

Always assess the risks you identify in a consistent way. This will allow you to prioritize them and decide which risk should be acted upon first.

> **TOP TIP**
>
> If any of the risks you identify rate as being 'high'
> probability AND 'high' impact, you should probably
> stop the project – or at least make very careful
> contingency plans!

Record the risk and take corrective action

Once you've assessed the risks you face, you can look
at ways of managing them. When you're doing this, it
is important to choose solutions that won't cost the
earth; in most cases, there's no point in spending more
money to eliminate a risk than the cost of the event if
it occurs.

Risk may be managed in a number of ways:

✓ By using existing assets. Here, existing resources
   can be used to counter risk. This may involve
   improvements to existing methods and systems,
   changes in responsibilities, improvements to
   accountability and internal controls, etc.

✓ By contingency planning. You may decide to
   accept a risk, but choose to develop a plan to
   minimize its effects. A good contingency plan
   will allow you to take action immediately and
   effectively with the minimum of project control.

✓ By investing in new resources. Your risk analysis
   should give you the basis for deciding whether to
   bring in additional resources to counter the risk.

In practice, new risks will nearly always appear as you
progress, and it is therefore essential that a review

of the risks is completed at each stage of the project lifecycle.

Keep your risks in a list or 'risk log' as follows, so that you can keep track of each one:

- date;

- description of risk;

- probability (H/M/L) and impact (H/M/L);

- who is responsible for resolution of risk;

- action being taken to resolve the risk;

- next review date or date for resolution.

TOP TIP

Remember that sometimes it may, in fact, be better to accept a risk than to use excessive resources to eliminate it. Keep calm and think through a problem carefully before you act.

Step three:
Stay in control of changes

Another factor that can affect your project, or even derail it, is change – either alterations that are requested by someone with influence (your main customer for example) or those that are due to unforeseen circumstances.

When faced with changes, it's worth remembering the triangle diagram of the project parameters that was discussed in Chapter 1 (see p. 13). Any change that affects one of the three parameters – time, cost or quality – is likely to have an impact on the other two. For example:

- a quality issue is likely to require increased cost and/or time to correct;

- resolving a time delay will either increase costs or compromise quality.

It's very important, then, to look closely at any proposed change before you throw yourself into it. Make sure you define it, mull it over and get it approved. All of this will minimize the effect the change may have on the rest of the project.

Any request or actions taken should be recorded in a 'change log' similar to the 'risk log' described in Step two. There are four stages to change management.

1. Propose a change

This process enables anyone within the team (including stakeholders or customers) to propose a change to a project. The proposal must include a description of the change and the reason for making it, and it should be formally presented using some sort of 'change request' form.

2. Summarize the impact

This is carried out by the project manager, who logs the change and considers the overall impact on the project. You should think about the following in your assessment, before recommending whether or not the change should be made:

- quantifiable cost savings and/or benefits;

- estimated cost;
- impact on timescales;
- additional resources required;
- impact on other projects and activities;
- additional risk and issues.

3. Make a decision

If the request is for major change, it should then be reviewed by an approved authority (such as the project sponsor), who will consider all of the information provided by the person making the request and the project manager.

4. Make the change

If the change is approved, it is scheduled, implemented and removed from the change log.

TOP TIP

Don't be afraid to reject a change request if you think it'll threaten the successful completion of your project – you're quite within your rights.

For example, say your project relates to moving offices. At a late stage, one company director wants the new offices to be repainted in colours that reflect your corporate logo, although they have already been painted white. There is no commercial reason for the request, and the likely impact would be to blow your budget and delay the move.

You assess the request and say 'no'.

Common mistakes

✗ You get paralyzed with nerves

Having received all these dire warnings about things that can go wrong, it's important that you remember that there's also such a thing as worrying too much. Don't be afraid to fail or you'll never succeed! If you create sufficient contingency plans and alternative approaches for the items or plans that are high risk, you'll be fine.

✗ You decide that the control processes are simply too much

It can be tempting to feel that formal risk and change management processes belong in the category of 'taking a sledgehammer to crack a nut'. Skimping on them, however, is asking for trouble. If you put them in place from the start, you'll be doing yourself a huge favour by cutting out your biggest potential source of stress.

BUSINESS ESSENTIALS

✓ Plan, plan and plan your project, using your whole project team so that they are on board and can contribute their experience and expertise.

✓ Identify, evaluate and manage any potential risks that may threaten the success of your project, remembering that some risks may have to be lived with if fixing them means they are too expensive to cut out altogether.

✓ Control any changes that have to be made for any reason by assessing and evaluating their impact. Don't be afraid to refuse changes if their knock-on effects on the rest of the project are too heavy.

✓ Don't get so worried that you become paralyzed. Good contingency planning will give you sufficient leeway should the odd mistake creep in here and there.

✓ Don't skimp on the control processes, even for a small project.

Where to find more help

Online and educational training will help you expand your project-managing skills and give you access to resources, as will the thousands of tutorials, guides, blogs, forums and podcasts on the Internet. For practical aids, there are many software packages on the market to keep any project on track no matter how complicated; most are subscription-based but some offer free templates. For further reading, below are a few of the publications that can help round out your knowledge of project management.

Podcasts and blogs

Andy Kauffman's People and Projects Podcast: www.peopleandprojectspodcast.com

Cornelius Fichtner: www.project-management-podcast.com

Project Management Paradise Podcast: www.projectmanagementparadise.com

Ricardo Vargas's 5 Minutes Podcast: ricardo-vargas .com/podcasts

Project Manager's Hacks: www.projectmanagementhacks.com

Project Manager's Tips: pmtips.net

Software and templates

asana.com

clickup.com

monday.com

projectmanagement.com

www.projectmanagementdocs.com

www.smartsheet.com

trello.com

www.wrike.com

Publications

The Economist Guide to Change and Project Management. Paul Roberts. The Economist, 2020.

A clear and structured approach to ensure projects not only run to budget and schedule, but also successfully deliver.

The PMBOK Guide, Seventh Edition. Project Management Institute, 2021.

An essential resource by the PMI, this is more than just a study guide for those taking the PMP and CAPM certifications. It sets the standard for best practices and resources.

Project Management All-in-One for Dummies. Stanley Portny. For Dummies, 2020.

A seven-book compilation of hands-on information and advice to organize, plan and execute your projects.

Project Management Handbook: How to Launch, Lead and Sponsor Successful Projects. Antonio Nieto-Rodriguez. Harvard Business Review, 2021.

In practical, non-technical language, this book breaks down any project into essential building blocks that can be easily understood by all project stakeholders and includes case studies from many varied industries.

Scrum: The Art of Doing Twice the Work in Half the Time. Jeff Sutherland. Random House Business, 2015.

A specific framework for accomplishing complex projects quickly.

Index

BUSINESS ESSENTIALS